D1100910

THE M. & E. HANDBOOK SERIES

STATISTICS

THE M. & E. HANDBOOK SERIES

STATISTICS

W. M. HARPER, A.C.W.A., A.M.B.I.M.
Senior Lecturer at the City of London College

MACDONALD & EVANS LTD
8 John Street, London W.C.1
1965

First published October 1965
Reprinted March 1966
Reprinted October 1966
Reprinted September 1967
Reprinted May 1968
Reprinted (with amendments) March 1969
Reprinted August 1970

©

MACDONALD & EVANS LTD
1965

S.B.N.: 7121 1910 8

Printed in Great Britain by
UNWIN BROTHERS LIMITED
WOKING AND LONDON

HL 8372

GENERAL INTRODUCTION

The HANDBOOK Series of Study Notes

HANDBOOKS are a new form of printed study notes designed to help students to prepare and revise for professional and other examinations. The books are carefully programmed so as to be self-contained courses of tuition in the subjects they cover. For this purpose they comprise detailed notes, self-testing questions and, hints on examination technique.

HANDBOOKS can be used on their own or in conjunction with recommended text-books. They are written by college lecturers, examiners and others with wide experience of students' difficulties and requirements. At all stages the main objective of the authors has been to prepare students for the practical business of passing examinations.

P. W. D. REDMOND
General Editor

NOTICE TO LECTURERS

Many lecturers are now using **HANDBOOKS** as working texts to save time otherwise wasted by students in protracted note-taking. The purpose of the series is to meet practical teaching requirements as far as possible, and lecturers are cordially invited to forward comments or criticisms to the Publishers for consideration.

AUTHOR'S PREFACE

STATISTICS is a subject that needs, above all, an understanding of the reasons for adopting the procedures employed and accepting the conclusions drawn. The purpose of this book is to give the student who initially knows nothing of statistics this understanding in order that he will be able to take intermediate professional examinations in the subject with success.

It has been my experience that excessive qualification of statements or completely rigorous definitions, though appropriate for the expert, serve only to confuse the student whose object at this stage is wisely limited to grasping the basic principles. Since student comprehension has been my dominant aim throughout this book, I have endeavoured to avoid such confusion.

Topics to be studied

Not all examining bodies examine on exactly the same topics. The student should ascertain by means of syllabuses and past examination questions exactly which ones he must prepare. The division of the book into parts, chapters and sections will then enable him to select easily those particular topics for detailed study.

Answers to Progress Tests

Answers to most of the questions in the Progress Tests are given either at the end of the question concerned or in Appendix IV, "Suggested answers." Where for reasons of space it has not been practical to supply any answer at all, the question is marked with an asterisk (*).

Decimal currency. This book follows the recommendations of the various accountancy bodies and of the examining bodies responsible for National Further Education syllabuses and examinations, and gives decimal currency equivalents where appropriate. These are set out in the form advised by the Decimal Currency Board, as described in *Decimal Currency: Expressions of Amounts in printing, writing and in speech,* H.M.S.O., 1968.

Bibliography

For further study, the student is referred to the following books:

Freund and Williams, *Modern business statistics* (Pitman).

For a more detailed exposition, moving on to some advanced topics: Wallis and Roberts, *Statistics—a new approach* (Methuen).

For more detailed discussion on statistical data (*e.g.* economics, social and vital statistics, and surveys): A. R. Illersic, *Statistics* (HFL Publishers Ltd).

For more emphasis on the mathematical aspects of statistics: Brookes and Dick, *Introduction to statistical method* (Heinemann).

For a popular book on the use of statistics—which also goes beyond the present work: M. J. Moroney, *Facts from figures* (Pelican).

For the next step: R. Goodman, *Teach yourself statistics* (English Universities Press).

And a highly recommended, light but informative book on the interpretation of statistics: D. Huff, *How to lie with statistics.*

For fuller treatment of index numbers: W. R. Crowe, *Index numbers: theory and applications* (Macdonald & Evans).

And for further reading: G. L. Thirkettle, *Wheldon's Business statistics* (Macdonald & Evans).

Acknowledgments

I gratefully acknowledge permission to quote from the past examination papers of the following bodies:

British Institute of Management (B.I.M.).

Building Societies Institute (B.S.I.).

London Chamber of Commerce (L.C.C.).

Local Government Examinations Board (L.G.E.B.).

Union of Lancashire & Cheshire Institutes (H.L.C.I.).

Institute of Hospital Administrators (I.H.A.).

Royal Society of Arts (R.S.A.).

Institute of Cost and Works Accountants (I.C.W.A.).

Association of Certified and Corporate Accountants
(A.C.C.A.).
University of London (B.Sc.).
Northern Counties Technical Examination Council
(N.C.T.E.C.).
Institute of Transport (I.O.T.).
Institute of Marketing and Sales Management (I.M.S.M.).

In addition I would particularly like to thank my colleague,
Mr L. Stafford, for his very considerate advice at all stages, and
Mrs Margaret Millar-Rae for her competent handling of the
secretarial work.   Their assistance proved invaluable and a
major factor in the preparation of this book.

July 1965; January 1969   W. M. H.

CONTENTS

xi

CONTENTS

LIST OF ILLUSTRATIONS

LIST OF TABLES

PART ONE

INTRODUCTION TO STATISTICS

CHAPTER I

NATURE AND INTERPRETATION OF STATISTICS

SECTION 1.   NATURE OF STATISTICS

1. What is statistics? Definitions differ, but essentially statistics is a scientific approach to information presenting itself in numerical form which enables us to maximise our understanding of such information.

The figures which result from statistical analysis are also referred to as "statistics." But the subject of statistics is wider than this, and can be divided into two parts:

(a) *Descriptive* statistics, dealing with methods of *describing a large mass of data.*

(b) *Analytical* statistics, dealing with methods that *enable a conclusion to be drawn* from the data.

2. Importance of statistics. Only recently has it been realised that society need not be run on the basis of hunches or trial and error. The development of statistics has shown that many aspects of progress depend on the correct analysis of numerical information—particularly in economics and commerce. Increasingly *figures* have become the basis of rational decisions (rather than hunches) and events are proving that these decisions based on figures give better results.

All this has led to an unprecedented demand for figures—a sort of "numbers explosion." But figures have to be understood and correctly handled, and this is the task of statistics. It is a task that will grow rapidly in importance—in business, in government and in science. It may even be one of the factors which determine the future rate of human progress.

3. Plan of this book. The book is arranged in logical sequence:

Part One: Basic concepts of statistics.

Part Two: Collection and presentation of figures which form the basis of statistical analysis.

Part Three: Different ways of presenting and describing a collection of figures relating to a single characteristic.

Part Four: Techniques for determining the relationship between two series of figures.

Part Five: The technique of drawing conclusions about a whole population from a relatively small sample—vital in modern statistics.

Part Six: Index numbers and time series.

Finally there are appendixes, a list of essential formulae, a collection of past examination questions, and suggested answers to certain questions in the Progress Tests.

4. Variables. In statistics, numbers are used to measure characteristics, *e.g.* height, weight, time, money, the number of marriages or houses, the number of blue-eyed males in France, etc.

A characteristic that is being measured is called a "variable." Thus, if we are measuring the weights of children, then "weights of children" is the variable.

There is no restriction on the number of variables we must have in any statistical analysis, though of course there must be at least one. In this book most of our attention will be directed to single variable analyses, though two-variable problems (such as the relationship between advertising and sales) is the basis of the whole of Part Four.

SECTION 2. INTERPRETATION OF STATISTICS

1. Danger of wrong interpretation. One of the first things that students of statistics must recognise is that figures can very easily be interpreted wrongly. Sayings such as "You can prove anything with figures" have gained widespread circulation because they embody the bitter experience of people who have found themselves misled by incorrect deductions drawn from basically correct figures.

Consequently many people tend to distrust statistics, and to regard statisticians as naive and incautious. In fact, statisticians are trained:

(a) *to be extremely careful in selecting information* on which to base their calculations; *see* "Biased sources," 2 below.

(b) *to make only such deductions as are strictly logical; see* "Invalid arguments," 3 below.

2. Biased sources.

One of the chief dangers facing a statistician is that the sources of his information may be biased. A statistician must therefore always ask himself such questions as:

(a) *Who* says this?
(b) *Why* does he say it?
(c) *What does he stand to gain* from saying it?
(d) *How* does he *know*?
(e) Could he be *lying*? Or *guessing*?

EXAMPLES

(1) A politician might say, "Seventy-five per cent of the votes were cast for me. This means that most people in this constituency want me as their MP." But what if less than two-thirds of the electorate voted?

(2) "Nine out of ten TV stars genuinely believe our product the best." But did they choose their ten stars carefully?

(3) "Nobody has put forward a justifiable complaint about our products." Who decides what is justifiable?

3. Invalid arguments.

A source of information may be completely unbiased, and yet faulty reasoning produce a completely invalid argument based upon it. Statisticians, therefore, are much concerned to ensure that their deductions are strictly logical.

EXAMPLES

(1) A politician might say, "My party has doubled its votes since the last election, and this proves that its support is greater than ever." But his party may have trebled the number of candidates it put up since the last election. Or the last election may have produced an abnormally low poll.

(2) "This penny has come down heads five times running. The chances are in favour of it coming down tails at the next toss." This is not so. The laws of probability give tails a 50/50 chance at every toss, no matter what sequence preceded it.

(3) "More people were hurt in the home than in factories and mines. Homes are therefore more dangerous than factories and mines."

Sometimes the fallacy in an argument is easier to detect if one asks oneself: is there any other possible explanation?

EXAMPLES

(1) "Hospital records show that the number of people being treated for this disease has doubled in the last twenty years. Therefore twice as many people suffer from the disease now." Possibly, but the figures may merely indicate that more people now take hospital treatment for the disease, or that methods of diagnosis have improved.

(2) "Last year 700 employees produced 150,000 ladders. This year 650 employees produced 160,000 ladders. This shows we have increased our productivity." Or alternatively we may have decreased our ladder sizes!

SECTION 3. THE MATHEMATICAL LANGUAGE OF STATISTICS

1. Mathematical language. The main purpose of a language is to enable people to exchange ideas with the minimum effort and maximum clarity. Mathematics has its own language, with a vocabulary of its own (symbols), for the purpose of communicating mathematical ideas.

The mere sight of mathematical expressions is often enough to make students shy away from what appears to them incomprehensible. But mathematical language is actually very easy to learn, and the few symbols explained below are enough to make the mathematical parts of this book fully intelligible.

Mathematics is particularly suitable as a language, as it often involves a series of operations, and the order of the operations can be indicated by the lay-out of the expression. For example, one important measure is the *standard deviation*, and the procedure for calculating it could be stated in writing thus: "To find the standard deviation, divide the number of items in the group into the sum of the squares of the differences between the value of each item in the group and the mean of the group—and then find the square root of this figure." How much easier and quicker it is to set out this statement in mathematical language:

$$\sigma = \sqrt{\frac{\Sigma (x - \bar{x})^2}{n}}$$

3. The language of statistics.*

"*Nouns*"

x This is a collective symbol meaning *all* the individual values of a variable. Strictly speaking, it stands for x_1 and x_2 and x_3, *etc.*, where x_1 is the first value in the group, x_2 the second, x_3 the third, *etc.*

y This is an alternative symbol to x. It is used where there are two sets of variables and x has already been used to indicate the first.

$\bar{x}$ (called "bar x"). A bar over a variable symbol indicates that it represents the *arithmetic mean* of the values of that variable.

f This stands for "frequency," *i.e.* the number of times a given value occurs in a collection of figures.

n This stands for the number of items (or pairs of items) in a collection of figures.

σ (called *sigma*). This stands for "standard deviation." A small suffix (*e.g.* σ_x; σ_y) indicates which variable it relates to.

d This stands for "deviation," and is the difference between two values—the appropriate values depending on the statistical technique being used.

r This stands for "coefficient of correlation."

r' This stands for "coefficient of rank correlation."

$\simeq$ This means "approximately equals."

" *Verbs*"

Σ (also called *sigma*; it is the capital letter version of σ). This means "the sum of" and simply indicates that the numbers following it should be added. For example, Σx means: "Add up all the values in the group relating to the x variable." If the group is 6, 8 and 15, then Σx is $6 + 8 + 15 = 29$. Sometimes before adding we must perform a prior operation, such as multiplying or subtracting.

If multiplying, the symbols to be multiplied are

---

* The student need not concern himself unduly if he cannot follow some of the explanations to the symbols at first reading. When the work involving these symbols is covered later in the book their meaning will be much clearer.

written together with the Σ sign in front, *e.g.* Σxy means *first* multiply each pair of x and y's and *then add* the products.

If subtracting, a bracket is put round the symbols to be subtracted and the Σ sign written *outside* the bracket, *e.g.* $\Sigma(x - \bar{x})$ means *first* subtract $\bar{x}$ from each x and then add.

Finally, note that Σx^2 means "Square each x figure first, then add," while $(\Sigma x)^2$ means "Add the x's first, then square the sum."

It is *very* important that operations are done in their correct order.

Suffixes

Small suffixes to symbols are used for identification in cases where the symbol may be used in more than one context.

Index number symbols

In addition to the other symbols, index numbers use a few more of their own:

p Price of individual items.

p_0 Price of individual items in base year.

p_1, p_2, p_3, *etc.*   Prices of individual item in subsequent years.*

q Quantity of individual items.

q_0 Quantity of individual items in base year.

q_1, q_2, *etc.*   Quantities of individual items in subsequent years.*

w Weight.

Note that Σpq means that the price and quantity of each item in turn are first multiplied together and the products then added.

4. Example of interpretation. To demonstrate the interpretation of this language the following important formula will be analysed:

$$r = \frac{\Sigma xy - n\,\bar{x}\,\bar{y}}{n\sigma_x\,\sigma_y}$$

This means that r, the coefficient of correlation, is found by the following calculation:

* If the current year only is being compared with base year, then the suffix indicates the current year.

(a) Multiply each x and y together and then add the products (Σxy).

(b) Next subtract from this figure the product of: the number of pairs of items; the arithmetic mean of the x variables; and the arithmetic mean of the y variables.

(c) Finally divide the answer by the product of: the number of pairs of items; the standard deviation of the x values; and the standard deviation of the y values.

PROGRESS TEST 1

1. Consider the following statements critically:*

(a) "Five years ago the average stay of patients in this hospital was 21 days—now it is only 16 days. This shows that we now cure our patients more quickly."

(b) "Most car accidents occur within five miles of the driver's home. Therefore long journeys are safer."

(c) "Ten per cent of the drivers involved in car accidents had previously taken X. A parallel survey of drivers *not* involved in accidents showed that only 1% had taken X. This shows that taking X is a contributory cause of accidents."

CHAPTER II

ACCURACY AND APPROXIMATION

SECTION 4. ACCURACY

1. Accuracy. Complete accuracy in statistics is often impossible owing to:

(a) *Inaccurate figures.* In statistics it is only rarely that completely accurate figures can be used. For example, if articles are weighed there is a limit to accuracy of the scales. Or when a count is made, there may be an element of doubt. Thus, however carefully a census is carried out there are always some people omitted for one reason or another who should have been included, and so the final figure is not completely accurate.

(b) *Incomplete data.* Complete accuracy is also impossible where calculations are made from data lacking all the necessary information. For example, in a later chapter we shall discuss the calculation of an average from data where individual values are not given, only the number of items which fall within a given range. Such an average figure must inevitably be only an approximation—albeit a very close approximation—to the true figure.

2. Spurious accuracy. It is not enough merely to appreciate that complete accuracy is usually impossible: it is also important that *no claim* should be made for such accuracy where it does not exist. Students may assert that they never do make such claims, but they should realise that every figure they write makes a statement regarding the accuracy of that figure.

For example, to write $4 \cdot 286$ means that an accuracy of up to three decimal places is being claimed. It *must* mean that, for if the accuracy is only to two decimal places then the 6 is a wild guess, in which case it is pointless to include it. But since it *is* included, a reader will assume it does have meaning and that the writer of the figure is therefore claiming an accuracy of three decimal places.

From all this it follows that a figure should include only those digits which are accurate—otherwise a greater accuracy is implied than the figure really possesses. When a figure implies an accuracy greater than it really has, such accuracy is termed *spurious accuracy*. Not only is spurious accuracy pointless, but it can also mislead—sometimes seriously.

For instance, if a manufacturer is told that the estimated cost of an article is 26*s*. 6*d*. and he signs a contract to sell a quantity at 30*s*. each, he may regret his action when he learns that the cost price was based on an estimate of £4 for making three—give or take £1.

3. Slide-rule accuracy. The accuracy of a slide rule is limited to three or, at best, four significant figures (for the meaning of *significant figure, see s*. **5.** 2). However, since complete accuracy is rarely possible in statistics, this limitation is usually of little consequence. Since calculations are made much more quickly and easily with a slide rule, students are strongly recommended to use one for all statistical work—in fact, all but the simplest calculations in this book have been carried out on such a rule.

NOTE: The use of slide rules is usually allowed in examinations, though it may be as well to indicate where they have been employed by adding the note "*Slide rule accuracy*" to the answer.

SECTION 5. APPROXIMATION

1. Rounding. If *some* figures in a survey will not be accurate, there is little point in recording the other figures with absolute accuracy. Consequently, when such figures are collected they are frequently *rounded*. For instance, in a survey of petrol sold at petrol stations the recorded figures may be rounded to the complete gallon, to tens of gallons or even to hundreds of gallons. This means making a decision as to *how* to round the actual detailed figures.

There are three methods of rounding:

   (a) *Round up.*—Thus if figures are to be rounded by raising them to the next ten gallons, an actual figure of 185 would be recorded as 190.

   (b) *Round down.*—Conversely, the figure can be rounded by reducing it to the previous ten. In that case 185 would be recorded as 180.

(c) *Round to the nearest unit.*—The figure can be rounded
to the nearest ten. The rule for a figure exactly half
way between, such as 185, is round so that the rounded
figure is an even unit. Rounding 185 to the nearest ten
means we must choose between 18 tens (180) or 19 tens
(190). The rule says choose the even—18 tens,
180.

NOTE: Rounding up and rounding down are not recommended
in statistics, as they give rise to what is known as *systematic
bias*. In rounding up, a little is added to every figure, so that
the ultimate total could be very much greater than the true
total. Similarly, rounding down gives a total smaller than the
true one. With rounding to the nearest unit, though, the small
amounts added tend to balance out the small amounts deducted
and the ultimate total is closer to the true total.

2. Significant figures. This term often crops up when
accuracy is under discussion. *Significant figures* are the digits
that carry real information and are free of spurious accuracy.
How many digits are in fact significant in any individual
amount depends on the degree of rounding that may have
occurred at some earlier stage in the calculations. The
concept is perhaps best grasped by means of examples:

	Stated figure when accuracy is known to be to:		
Calculated figure	*4 significant figures*	*3 significant figures*	*2 significant figures*
613·82	613·8	614	610
0·002817	0·002817	0·00282	0·0028
3,572,841	3,573,000	3,570,000	3,600,000
40,000	40,000	40,000	40,000

It should be noted that zeros which only indicate the *place
value* of the significant figure (*e.g.* tens, hundreds, thousands)
are not counted as significant digits.

3. Adding and subtracting with rounded numbers. When
adding or subtracting with rounded numbers it is important
to remember that the answer cannot be more accurate than
the least accurate figure.

EXAMPLE

Add 225, 541 *and* 800, *where the* 800 *has been rounded to the nearest* 100.

$225 + 541 + 800 = 1,566$. But since the least accurate figure is to the nearest 100, the answer must also be given only to the nearest 100, *i.e.* 1,600. Any attempt to be more exact can only result in spurious accuracy (indeed, even the 6 in 1,600 is suspect, for since 800 is subject to be possible error of 50 either way, the true answer lies between 1,516 and 1,616; *i.e.* 1,500 may easily be a more accurate rounded figure than 1,600).

4. Multiplying and dividing with rounded numbers. When multiplying or dividing with rounded numbers, ensure that the answer does not contain more significant figures than any of the *rounded* figures used in the calculation.

EXAMPLE

(1) *Multiply* $1 \cdot 62$ *by* $3 \cdot 2$ (*both rounded*).

$1 \cdot 62 \times 3 \cdot 2 = 5 \cdot 184$. But since $3 \cdot 2$ is only two significant figures the answer can only contain two significant figures, *i.e.* $5 \cdot 2$.

(2) *Multiply* $1 \cdot 62$ *by* 2, *where* 2 *is an exact* (i.e. *not a rounded*) *figure*.

$1 \cdot 62 \times 2 = 3 \cdot 24$. Since $1 \cdot 62$ is correct to three significant figures, the answer can be left as three figures (but note that the 4 is still suspect. The $1 \cdot 62$ could represent any figure between $1 \cdot 615$ and $1 \cdot 625$. These doubled are $3 \cdot 23$ and $3 \cdot 25$—either of which may be closer the true answer than our $3 \cdot 24$).

5. Maximums and minimums. The above rules are easy to remember and while usually quite suitable in practice are not always free from possible slight error—as has been demonstrated. If an *error-free* figure is required then the following procedure should be followed:

(a) Re-write each rounded figure twice—first giving it the *maximum* value it could represent, and then giving it the *minimum*.

(b) Next calculate two answers: one using the maximums and the other the minimums. The true figure should be stated as lying between these two answers.

EXAMPLE

Add 15·04, 21 and 10·3 (all rounded numbers).

Maximums	Minimums
15·045	15·035
21·500	20·500
10·350	10·250
46·895	45·785

Therefore the true answer lies between **45·785** and **46·895**.

This can be alternatively stated as 46·340 ± 0·555 (46·340 being the midpoint of 45·785 and 46·895).

6. Absolute and relative error. The actual amount of an error is termed the *absolute error*. However, we are often not so much concerned with the actual amount of an error as with the size of the error relative to the total figure. Thus in measuring the distance between London and Sydney, an error of a mile is insignificant, whereas such an error in the distance between Dover and Calais would be serious. Consequently, computing the percentage that the absolute error bears to the total figure gives a measure of the *relative* error.

$$\text{Therefore } Relative\ error = \frac{Absolute\ error}{Estimated\ figure} \times 100$$

EXAMPLE

Find the maximum relative error of the previous Example.

$$Relative\ error = \frac{0·555}{46·34} \times 100 = 1·2\%.$$

PROGRESS TEST 2

(Answers on page 249)

1. Add: 280 tons; 500 tons; 641 tons; 800 tons; 900 tons.

2. 1,200 people (to the nearest 100) were found to buy a sack of potatoes every quarter. Each sack weighed 112 lb. (to the nearest lb.). Calculate the total weight of potatoes bought in a year.

3. Add the following rounded figures and state the answer *as accurately as possible*, on the assumption that (a) rounding was to the nearest digit, (b) the figures were rounded *up*: 2·81; 4·373; 9·2; 5·005.

PART TWO

THE COMPILATION AND PRESENTATION
OF STATISTICS

CHAPTER III

COLLECTION OF DATA

Before any statistical work can be done at all, figures must be collected. The collection of figures is a very important aspect of statistics since any mistakes, errors or bias which arise in collection will be reflected in conclusions subsequently based on such figures.

Always remember that *a conclusion can never be better than the original figures on which it is based.* Unless the original figures are collected properly, any subsequent analysis will be, at best, a waste of time and possibly even disastrous, since it may mislead, with serious consequences.

SECTION 6. POPULATION AND SAMPLE

1. Alternatives. Two methods are open to us in collecting data. The figures can be collected from:

(a) the entire *population*, or
(b) a *sample* of the population.

First, though, these terms should be explained.

2. Population. This is a technical term in statistics with the specific meaning of the entire body of items about which we want to obtain information. For example, if we wish to know what proportion of doctors in the U.K. watch television, then our "population" will be all the doctors in the U.K. If we wish to know the colour of all the cars on English roads, our population is all the cars on English roads. Note that this is *not* the same as all English cars: some cars on English roads may be foreign. It is very important that the population should be carefully defined.

For instance, in an inquiry relating to the number of house-wives who go out to work, how should "housewife" be defined? If it is taken to mean a wife with no occupation other than housekeeping, the survey would show that *no* housewives go out to work! If it means a wife who keeps house, then the question arises whether a newly-wed in a one-room flat with her husband away on business nearly all the time is really a "housewife." And should we include the wife who has a maid to do most of the housework? Different interpretations will lead to different results in the analysis.

Another problem sometimes associated with the population is that its full extent may not be known; for example, the number of people in England with unsuspected diabetes. Obviously it is not easy to collect figures for such a population.

To sum up, it should be clear that, before any figures are collected at all, careful consideration should be given to the population of any proposed survey.

3. Samples. Very often it is impracticable to obtain information on every item in the population and we have to be satisfied with a fraction of all such items. Such a fraction is known as a sample.

A *sample*, then, is a group of items taken from the population for examination.

SECTION 7. METHODS OF COLLECTION

1. Methods outlined. We have seen that figures relating to a chosen population can be obtained either from the whole population or from a sample. Whichever approach is decided on, one or a combination of the following methods can be adopted:

(a) *Direct observation.*—For example, counting for oneself the number of cars in a car park.
(b) *Interviewing.*—Asking personally for the required information.
(c) *Abstraction from published statistics.*
(d) *Postal questionnaire.*—Sending a questionnaire by post and requesting completion.

2. Direct observation. This is the best method, as it reduces the chance of incorrect data being recorded. Unfortunately it cannot always be used, generally on account of the cost. It would be uneconomical, for instance, to follow a housewife